DECOUPAGE

The Decorative Workshop

DECOUPAGE

A Practical
Step-by-Step Guide

JOANNA JONES

FRIEDMAN/FAIRFAX
PUBLISHERS

A FRIEDMAN/FAIRFAX BOOK

© 1993 Merehurst Ltd

Published in1995 by Michael Friedman Publishing Group, Inc.
by arrangement with
Merehurst Ltd
Ferry House
51-57 Lacy Road
Putney   London
SW15 1PR

Library of Congress Cataloging-in-Publication Data

Jones, Joanna, date
   Découpage / Joanna Jones.
      p.   cm. — (The Decorative Workshop)
   "Originally published as Decorative découpage"—T.p. verso.
   Includes index.
   ISBN 1-56799-152-1 (paperback)
   ISBN 1-56799-191-2 (hardcover)
   1. Decoupage   I. Title.   II. Series.
TT870.J665   1995
745.54'6—dc20

                               94-27978
                                    CIP

Editor: Miren Lopategui
Designer: Maggie Aldred
Stylist: Joanna Jones
Photographer: Jon Bouchier

Originally published as *Decorative Découpage*

Typeset by J&L Composition Ltd
Color separations by Global Colour
Printed in Singapore by C.S. Graphics

For bulk purchases and special sales, please contact:
Friedman/Fairfax Publishers
Attention: Sales Department
15 West 26th Street
New York, NY 10010
212/685-6610 FAX 212/685-1307

Contents

Introduction

The first piece of decoupage I ever saw was a black letter rack, smothered in a gorgeous design of primroses and bluebells that had been cleverly balanced by softly colored flying birds. The decorative impact of the whole thing was nothing short of mouthwatering, while the finish on it was so perfect that I thought for a while it had been hand-painted.

For years I made this black letter rack my yardstick and would not accept anything less perfect from either myself or my students until, one day, I saw an eighteenth-century Italian cupboard at a very prestigious antiques exhibition. It was decorated with a decoupaged design, cut from contemporary hand-colored prints. The paintwork, which was cream and turquoise, was in good condition considering its age, but the prints were badly cut out, very sketchily colored, and had only the thinnest layer of varnish over them. What really amazed me, however, was that in spite of all this, the overall effect was absolutely fabulous.

A tremendous amount has been written about the perfect decoupage technique, and, indeed, some of the projects in this book seek to attain the perfect finish. Since seeing that old cupboard, however, I am prepared to admit openly what I have always secretly suspected—that if your design has some panache and style, nobody is going to miss a few coats of varnish!

I am not saying that you should not cut out, color and glue as well as you possibly can, but don't let the whole thing become such a chore that you cease to enjoy it. If you enjoy, and are truly enthusiastic about, what you are doing, it gives the end result a glow and an attractiveness that just isn't there if you are laboriously going through the motions and have become bored.

HISTORY OF DECOUPAGE

If you look at the history of decoupage, you will realize that you are continuing a craft that goes back at least as far as the seventeenth century. The craving for chinoiserie was at its height then, and it was extremely important to get a perfect finish, in order to emulate the hand-painted and highly lacquered furniture that was coming into Europe from the Orient.

For various reasons, this highly sought-after furniture was arriving at far too slow a rate for the fashion-conscious, who simply had to have a piece in their homes. Luckily, the ever-helpful craftsmen of the day hit upon the comparatively speedy idea of hand-coloring prints with a Chinese theme, so that they could be cut out and stuck onto appropriately designed furniture. The prints were then sunk under layers of varnish until they were indistinguishable from freehand paintings.

As the same thing was also happening in Venice, decoupage soon not only became an acceptable alternative to hand-painting, but also began to filter through to the leisured classes as a new hobby.

Although we know that decoupage was all the rage at the French court in the 1780s, I still find it very hard to imagine the likes of Marie Antoinette and her contemporaries slapping on coat after coat of varnish in their elaborate clothes and coiffures. I have a similar problem with the delicate, wasp-waisted Victorian ladies, who are also known to have taken to decoupage in a very big way—their specialties were huge screens covered in specially produced pictures called "scraps." What I would like to know is, where did they actually do it?

It must have been in the potting shed— they simply couldn't have worked with glue and varnish in the middle of all those stuffed birds and horsehair settees!

The thing is, I don't think that Marie Antoinette or the Victorians cared too much about how many coats of varnish their designs had. They just thoroughly enjoyed the whole process, and it shows in the wonderful designs they produced.

I would like you to really enjoy decoupage, too, and not to let yourself worry too much about the correctness of everything you do. If you want to go for a lacquer-like finish that has been achieved with 30 coats of varnish, that's wonderful, but if you are quite happy with the result you get after only two or three layers, just don't feel guilty about it! Remember, *you* are the designer!

Decoupage equipment can be divided into two shopping lists. The contents of the first—glue, paint, brushes and varnishes, etc.—can be bought fairly quickly in most hardware stores. The second list can be filled at a more leisurely pace, and a more enjoyable time can be had unearthing unusual wrapping papers, old pieces to decorate, prints and old books.

Nothing on either list is difficult to find, but you might need to build another shelf in the garage to keep it all!

Equipment and materials

THE MOST OBVIOUS EQUIPMENT YOU WILL need, of course, is something to decorate. But this will present no problems, since almost anything can be decoupaged, no matter what its age or what it's made from. My own particular preference is for old items, which I generally find in junk shops and at antique markets, but craft shops are also an excellent source for suitable wooden and cardboard objects such as the hatboxes in this book.

By using fabric instead of paper, decoupage can be extended to decorating old wicker furniture as well as baskets, while there is no end to the "potichomanie" you can do on glass plates, lamps and dishes. The possibilities are, literally, endless. In this book, I have shown how you can use decoupage on walls, but there is no reason why you shouldn't also have a go at fitted furniture and floors. You could even rival the Sistine Chapel and have a few angels flying around the ceiling!

Once you have decided what to decoupage, you will then have to consider more specific equipment, as described below.

SOURCES FOR CUTOUTS

Wrapping paper is so luscious nowadays, and usually of such good quality, that it is tempting to look no further. However, there are so many other lovely designs tucked away in old children's books and gardening manuals—not to mention on calendars and posters—that if you keep your eyes open, you can soon amass quite a collection.

There are also now several decoupage resource books that provide a terrific selection of black-and-white and colored prints, which you can either cut out and use as they are, or have photocopied, enlarged or reduced, to use over and over again.

You don't even have to stick to pictures, because decorative maps, calligraphy, hieroglyphics or border patterns are all usable in various ways. In addition, the original, traditional Victorian paper scraps are actually being reprinted and are widely available in a variety of stores.

Avoid cutouts with heavy printing on the back of them. Although sealers will help a little, there is always a chance that the printing will show through and ruin your design.

BRUSHES

The golden rule for brushes is always to buy the best you can afford. You will be repaid by not having to stop constantly to fish out stray bristles from paint or varnish and by generally getting a much smoother finish.

House-painting brushes. I use ordinary 1- to 1½-inch (2.5–4cm) house-painting brushes for all oil-based paints.

Sable brushes. I use small sable brushes for painting with latex paint. These take some getting used to initially, as they are very soft and seem to have no "give," but they do leave a marvelously smooth finish.

Varnishing brushes. You can buy special varnishing brushes, but they are expensive and a small house-painting brush will do just as well, especially if you buy the fattest and silkiest one you can find. Once you have designated a brush for varnishing, however, you mustn't ever use it for anything else.

Artist's paintbrushes. If you are going to use your brush with acrylic paints, it is best to get one especially for this purpose, as acrylics are very hard on finer brushes such as sable. To mix up artist's oil colors, use an artist's ox-hair or camel-hair brush of a medium size.

GLUES

Polyvinyl acetate (PVA) or **white glue** is a flexible, reasonably fast-drying liquid glue that dries to a clear finish. For this reason, it is useful for gluing on the cutouts. It can also be diluted and used as a varnish, a stiffener and, to some extent, a sealer. Elmer's Glue-All is the best-known of the white glues.

Wood glue. I find that glue made specifically for wood is the answer to most wood sticking problems.

Spray adhesives are quick and very useful in some situations, but on the whole I prefer the messier and more versatile white glue.

PAINTS, PRIMERS AND UNDERCOATS

Primers. Use a wood primer on new or stripped wood to seal it and to prevent subsequent coats of paint from sinking into the grain. Give new unpainted metal, or metal that has been stripped, one or two coats of a bare metal primer such as red oxide.

Undercoats. It is always advisable to use an undercoat on new or stripped wood before applying the top coats. It is not always necessary if you are working on a sound painted or varnished surface, although it makes a useful first coat if you are painting onto a particularly intrusive color.

Latex paints. Latex paints are water-based and relatively quick-drying. Thinned down and built up in layers, they make a marvelous basis for decoupage. They are porous, however, and need to be sealed with an acrylic sealer before being decorated.

Oil-based household paints. Oil-based paints come in flat, satin (eggshell) and gloss finishes. Gloss paint is really not suitable for decoupage. Oil-based paints give a tougher finish than latex paints, and I like to use them on pieces that are likely to get a lot of wear and tear. Their only disadvantage is that you must allow twenty-four hours between applications.

Artist's oil paints. Artist's oil paints may be mixed with oil-based paints to tint them, but they are slow-drying and will slightly delay the drying time of the original paint. When they are used on their own to color cracks or make antiquing fluid, it is best to leave the finish for at least a couple of days, even if it feels dry to the touch.

Artist's acrylic paints. Artist's acrylic paints are usually bought in tubes, but now there are small containers of acrylic craft paints available, which come in a more fashionable range of colors and which you will find useful if you are not very good at mixing colors.

Acrylics are mixed with water and dry very quickly, although you can buy a retardant, which will slow down the drying time a little. They are very useful for putting the finishing touches on pieces of decoupage and may be applied over latex or oil-based paints.

Oil-based and watercolor pencils. Either of these may be used for coloring prints, although in the case of watercolor pencils, care must be taken not to get the print too wet, as it will tend to buckle. Pencils are also very useful for repairing any accidental damage that might occur during the rubbing-down process.

PAINT AND VARNISH REMOVERS

Paint and varnish removers are very caustic and are best applied with an old housepainting brush. Wear

rubber gloves and make sure that you follow the instructions on the container to the letter. The best type of tool to use is a pointed multi-edged paint scraper, which is made specifically for the job, although with some tricky corners anything that gets results is the best thing to use!

SANDPAPER AND STEEL WOOL

Sandpaper and steel wool are produced in all grades, from very fine to coarse. They are used at all stages of decoupage, from smoothing the initial surface to rubbing down the final layer of varnish.

I also find abrasive cloths and pads very useful, especially for rubbing down metal.

You may prefer to use wet-or-dry sandpaper for rubbing down wood, metal, or oil-based paint surfaces, but I do not advocate their wet use for a latex paint surface or for varnish that is covering prints, as it is difficult to see exactly what you are doing underneath all the "slurry."

KNIVES, SCISSORS, CUTTING BOARDS, AND ROLLERS

Knives. There are dozens of craft knives on the market, some cheap and disposable, others with a long strip of push-up blades that snap off when they need to be replaced. Most of these are not sharp enough or flexible enough for decoupage. The best one to get is an X-acto knife, a slim metal knife with sharp renewable blades that you must change the *minute* they start getting blunt.

Scissors. You will need a sharp curved pair of cuticle scissors, and once again, it is a question of buying the best you can afford. Sharpness is, of course, paramount, but you will also find that the more expensive scissors are more comfortable.

Comfort will definitely become a factor when you have been cutting for an hour or two!

Cutting boards. If you are using a knife to cut out your design, you will need a cutting board of some kind. The very best are made in Japan and are designed so that they literally "heal" themselves after you have cut on them. They are available in a variety of sizes from most good craft shops, but they are quite expensive.

Kitchen cutting boards or even old table mats make quite good alternatives, but you will have to stop using them as soon as they get scratched, or they will ruin your designs.

Rollers. A little rubber roller is very useful for going over larger cutouts in particular, as it ensures that no excess glue or air is trapped underneath and that everything is well glued.

SEALERS

Sealers have many uses. They are used on porous surfaces, such as latex paint or wood, to prevent subsequent layers of glue or varnish from sinking in. In addition, sealers are used to fix and seal hand-colored prints so that they do not run when they are glued and varnished. Finally, they are also used on all papers to make them less absorbent and to strengthen delicate designs during the cutting-out stage. Sealers are available in many forms. I find the acrylic spray-on variety the easiest to use.

TACK CLOTHS

Tack cloths are lint-free, extremely tacky cloths that will pick up all the dust and grit left behind by rubbing down with sandpaper. They are very easy to obtain now in hardware and paint stores and will make all the difference in the finish of your

work. Keep your tack cloth in a jar with a screw lid, and always shake it out well before using it. When using latex paint, use a lint-free cloth wrung out in warm water as a tack cloth.

Varnishes

The good news about varnishing is that it is the crowning glory of decoupage and, if well applied, provides that wonderful, luminous hand-painted quality. The bad news is that most varnishes have a yellowing effect on the underlying surface, which can be disappointing if you have chosen or matched your colors with care.

Polyurethane and spar varnish. I rather like the mellowing effect that polyurethane and spar varnishes give, and quite often emphasize it even more by antiquing the finished result. Polyurethane varnish will give you a really tough finish that will stand up to most household uses. It comes in a satin or gloss finish.

Spar varnish is even tougher and, for that reason, has the most yellowing effect. It comes only in a gloss finish.

Acrylic varnish. If you really want to keep as close to the original colors as possible, you can use an acrylic varnish, which, while it hardly discolors at all, is water-based and usually needs at least one coat of spar or polyurethane varnish to give it a tough enough finish for tables, trays and other commonly used surfaces. Acrylic varnish generally comes in a gloss or satin finish.

Crackle varnish gives your work a really cracked and ancient look, which looks particularly good over more classical designs. It is quite easy to obtain from most craft shops and art supply stores, and comes in a pack containing one bottle of fast-drying varnish and one bottle of slow-drying varnish, which is usually tinted to provide an even more antique effect.

Wax

A final coat or two of clear wax gives a lovely deep sheen to most pieces. I polish my work as often as possible, and the surface just keeps on getting better and better. Polishing with a high-quality tinted wax will also give your work quite a passable antiqued finish.

Solvents

Mineral spirits (odorless paint thinners) are substitutes for turpentine and may be used to dilute any oil-based paint and as a solvent for removing oil paint and polyurethane varnish from clothes and brushes. Mineral spirits may also be used with steel wool for rubbing down and cleaning old pieces that are about to be painted.

Denatured alcohol may be used with steel wool for rubbing down and cleaning. It is also useful for removing sticky layers of French polish.

Wood Fillers

Most quick-drying wood fillers will be suitable for anything that you are likely to come across in the way of holes, dents or cracks.

The secret to getting a really good finish is to make sure that you have everything you need before you start—and that includes adequate space and plenty of time.

There are no really difficult techniques in this book, but if, like me, you find that written instructions instantly make you feel inadequate, I suggest that you simply gather the materials together, clear your work space and get on with it.

Basic techniques

IT'S ALWAYS POSSIBLE TO BUY A NEW wooden or metal object to decoupage and to get right down to priming and painting. But if you can find an old piece with character, your decoupage will look a lot more exciting and authentic. However, there is always a downside to everything, and I'm afraid that if you are going for authenticity, before the pleasant tasks of applying colors and designs can begin, the more mundane jobs of stripping, rubbing down and filling must be tackled.

Although these jobs come pretty low on most people's list of favorite things, it can in fact be very satisfying to restore a rickety, battered and

heavily painted piece to its smooth, glued and wooden or metal origins before indulging in the ultimate pleasure of decorating.

STRIPPING

If you have a reasonably unbroken surface on the piece you wish to decorate, it is not always necessary to strip it, but if the paint or varnish is chipped and uneven, then it is a good idea to take it all off and start from scratch.

Basically, you have two choices when it comes to stripping: doing it yourself or taking it to a commercial stripper. The decision usually rests on how much money you wish to spend or how big the piece is. Taking the piece to a commercial stripper usually costs a lot more than doing it yourself, although, if it's a really big piece, it will certainly be a lot quicker—and they will usually pick up and deliver to your door.

Stripping at home

Stripping even small things at home can lead to chaos if you do not make adequate preparations. Stripping is not difficult in and of itself, but you do have to lock up any pets or small children, and make sure that everything that might get splashed is covered with a layer or two of newspaper. You should also wear an apron and a pair of rubber gloves.

There are several good brands of stripper or remover available that are suitable for either metal or wood, although you need to make sure that you get the correct one, depending on whether you are removing varnish or paint.

Incidentally, it is very easy to confuse a varnished surface with one that has been French-polished. If you are not sure, try rubbing a small corner of the surface with some fine steel wool soaked in denatured alcohol. If you are in fact dealing with

STRIPPING OFF PAINT

When using paint stripper, wear rubber gloves and make sure you follow the instructions on the container to the letter. The best type of tool to use is a pointed multi-edged paint scraper.

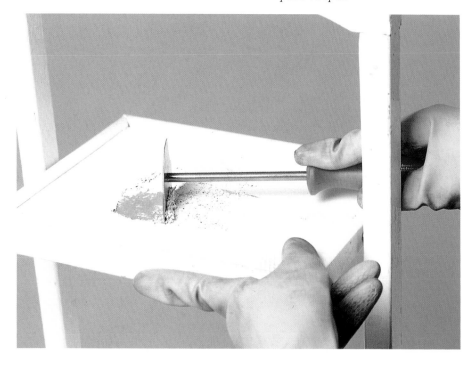

French polish, you will find that your steel wool will soon be clogged with a brown sticky mess, and you can continue to clean the rest of the French polish off with fresh applications of steel wool and denatured alcohol.

If the surface has been varnished, you will only remove the surface dirt with the steel wool and you will need to use a stripper specifically for varnished surfaces. Whichever type of surface you are removing, follow the instructions on the container carefully and allow it to dry.

Commercial stripping

If you decide to go for the commercial stripping option, you will find that you have a choice between the caustic and the non-caustic methods of stripping. There is quite a big difference between these two methods, in terms of both the actual process and the cost.

As usual, you get what you pay for, and you will find that the more expensive non-caustic method is the safest for anything delicate, such as pieces with gesso decoration or inlay, while the caustic method is more suitable for chunky pine pieces or cheap old "horrors" that you don't want to spend a fortune on.

Cleaning a sound surface prior to painting

If the surface you are going to decorate is absolutely sound, it will not need stripping, but it will need cleaning to remove any wax and dirt that might have collected over the years.

To remove wax, go over the whole piece with steel wool, soaked in mineral spirits. Rub with the grain whenever possible and replace the steel wool when it gets dirty. If you are quite sure that there is no wax or polish on the surface, you can just wipe it over with a cloth wrung out in hot soapy water. Be careful not to drench the piece in water, however, as this will raise the grain of

the wood and give you even more rubbing down to do!

GLUING AND FILLING

If you have any bits to glue back or holes to fill, this is the time to attend to them. As you may imagine, almost anything can happen to a piece of furniture over the years, and it would not be appropriate to deal with all the calamities here. However, for relatively simple problems such as replacing missing beading or reuniting split paneling, you will need a high-quality wood adhesive and clamps, pins, or even a heavy book or masking tape to hold the pieces together while they dry.

FILLING HOLES AND CRACKS

After cleaning old wooden furniture, fill in any holes with wood filler. When dry, rub down, first with medium sandpaper, then with fine, then "dust" with a tack cloth.

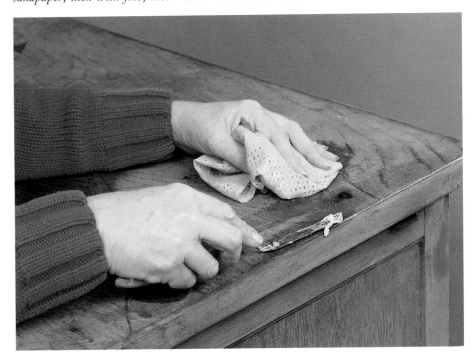

RUBBING WITH FINE STEEL WOOL

When you first start rubbing, you won't believe that it is possible to remove all the rust. Five minutes later, you may still not believe it. But you can and you must!

Wood filler can be used to fill holes and dents. It can also be used to give a smooth surface to a particularly rough-grained piece of wood or the rough ends of man-made boards, such as chipboard.

RUBBING DOWN

Whether your piece needs stripping or whether you are retaining the original surface, what you do next is of the utmost importance. If you don't make sure that you have a beautifully smooth surface at this point, you won't stand a chance of ending up with a perfect piece of decoupage, and all the painstaking work still to come will be wasted and made more difficult as a result.

Having thoroughly unnerved you with my last comment, let me tell you exactly how to achieve this beautifully smooth finish. First, when working with wood, use a sanding block whenever possible. Then, with sandpaper wrapped around the block, sand with long firm strokes, using your whole arm and shoulder and always going with the grain. Alternatively, you may prefer to use a good handful of very fine steel wool. I use fine sandpaper on large flat pieces and strips of steel wool for tricky pieces like turned legs and awkward corners. I also find fine abrasive cloths very flexible for anything with a rounded edge.

If you are decorating a metal piece, some of these cloths or pads are particularly useful, although very fine steel wool will also give metal a wonderful surface.

If your metal piece is old, it will almost certainly have developed some rust spots, which the stripping process will not remove entirely. Treat these with a rust remover and rub with a piece of fine steel wool until all traces of rust have been removed.

You may be tempted, especially on a large item, to use an electric sander, but unless you are particularly adept with this tool, I strongly advise you to resist the temptation. It is only too easy to overdo it and end up with disfiguring whirls in the wood, or very rough edges on the metal.

Whichever method you use to achieve your smooth surface, all will soon be lost if you do not make sure that you have cleaned away every speck of sawdust, dirt and other debris before continuing with the next stage.

The best way to ensure a dust-free surface is to wipe it carefully with a tack cloth. These are quite easy to obtain in hardware stores and are just what they sound—lint-free and extremely tacky rags.

If you make sure that you always replace tack cloths in their container or bag when you have finished with them and that you always give them a good shake before you use them again, they will last for ages. If, by any chance, you cannot track one down, any lint-free rag wrung out in turpentine (if you are using oil-based paints) or warm water (if you are using latex) will make a reasonable substitute.

PRIMING AND PAINTING

Priming metal

If you are working on old metal, you will have removed any trace of rust during the rubbing-down process. However, to ensure that your piece remains rust-free, you will need to prime it with two coats of a base metal primer such as red oxide before going any further.

If you are working on new metal, remove any superficial grease with hot soapy water and give the surface a slight roughness by rubbing it down with fine steel wool. Dry it well before applying metal primer.

Priming wood

If you are working on a rubbed-down surface that has already been painted or varnished, there will be no need to apply primer, but you will need to apply wood primer to anything that has been stripped or to new wood.

APPLYING THE BASE COAT

Painting with water-based paints

It is very difficult to say what the traditional base coat for decoupage is. Nowadays, you can find instructions that include only one coat of paint,

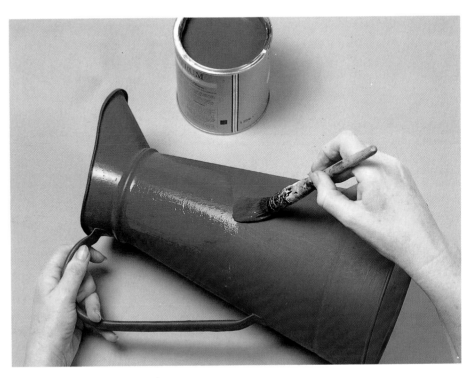

PRIMING WITH METAL PRIMER

Prime a metallic surface, inside and out, with two coats of a base metal primer such as red oxide. When dry, lightly rub down and wipe, then apply coats of thinned-down latex paint and acrylic sealer.

which is quite reasonable when you learn that eighteenth-century decoupeurs were known to stick their designs directly onto pasteboard.

I have always thought of the following method as being the traditional one. It is certainly the method that gives the most beautiful effect, although, I have to admit, it is also the one that requires the greatest amount of patience.

Pour some latex paint into a clean jar and dilute it with a little water (about a tablespoonful of water to half an average-sized jar). Stir the mixture well before applying it to the piece to be decorated,

using a soft sable brush, if possible (see "Brushes," page 10). If it is a wooden piece, paint in the same direction as the grain whenever possible, taking care to put on a thin, even coat of paint. Check for drips and let it dry.

Initially, you may put on two or even three of these thinned-down coats of paint before rubbing down gently with fine sandpaper and going over the piece with your tack cloth. Repeat this entire process, rubbing down and wiping between coats, until you have built up a smooth, even surface that is as close to alabaster as you can get!

Depending upon the make of paint you are using and your own personalized version of diluting,

COLORING A PRINT

First apply the color with watercolor pencils, then spread it with a damp brush so that it resembles watercolor. Be careful not to wet the print too much, or it will buckle.

this will probably involve between six and ten coats of paint. Finish by gently rubbing down and wiping the surface.

Painting with oil-based paints

I use oil-based paints as a base coat when I am doing a piece that is likely to get a lot of use and where latex paint would be more likely to chip. The best paint to use is one with a satin or eggshell finish. Generally speaking, it is not necessary to dilute it, although if you do need to, use the same method as for water-based paints, substituting turpentine or mineral spirits for water.

Use an ordinary 1- or 1½-inch (2.5 or 4 cm) house-painting brush and, as with latex, paint whenever possible in the direction of the grain.

You will find that oil-based paints take much longer to dry and that you will not usually need to apply more than three or four coats to achieve a good smooth surface. You will need to rub down and wipe after each coat.

You will find that I often say rub down "gently" and "lightly" in the projects. This is because once you have achieved your smooth surface prior to painting, all other rubbing down is simply to remove any slight irregularities, such as dust or brush marks. If you rub too hard, you will be back to the wood.

COLORING A PRINT

Nowadays, it is only too easy to go out and buy a couple of sheets of high-quality wrapping paper to cut out for decoupage, but in previous centuries decoupeurs used prints for their designs, some of which had to be colored before they could be used.

If you want to try your hand at coloring a print, first make sure that the print you have in mind is of no great value or, better still, acquire one of the excellent decoupage resource books that are available now. These contain dozens of copies of

the original colored and uncolored prints so that you can really make your piece look antique.

For coloring, use high-quality oil-based pencils so that you can mix them for maximum effect, and aim for plenty of variety in tone, leaving small amounts of white uncovered to keep the picture lively. It is not a good idea, however, to be too subtle, because very delicate colors will not show to advantage under several coats of varnish.

You will find that your pencils cover better and that you will have more control over gradations if you use short strokes packed close together. When you wish to shade a color gradually from light to dark, let longer and shorter strokes gently dovetail into one another where the light starts to merge into the dark. You will also get a more uniform effect if you keep your strokes going in the same direction as the original shading strokes on the print.

When you have completed the coloring stage of your print and before you cut it out, you will need to spray the right side sparingly with sealer (page 12) and let it dry.

If you are using watercolor pencils, apply the color dry in the usual way, spreading it with a damp brush so that it resembles watercolor. Take care not to wet the print excessively, for if you do it will buckle.

CUTTING OUT AND ARRANGING YOUR DESIGN

This is where the fun really begins, and I can honestly say that I know people who have become seriously addicted to the leisurely pursuit of cutting out designs for decoupage.

There are two ways of cutting: with a knife or with a small curved pair of cuticle scissors. I use both, depending on the intricacy of the design. There is nothing like a pair of scissors for swooping around the curved petals of a flower, but a knife is wonderful for tackling straight edges and slim stems.

Whichever method you decide upon, you will also need a larger pair of scissors to cut the print or paper into manageable pieces. Do not, for example, attempt to cut a tiny flower straight out of a whole sheet of wrapping paper.

If you are using a knife, work on a cutting board (page 12) and, whenever possible, move the paper rather than the knife, which should be cutting towards you. If you are using scissors, you will find it easier to work with your cutting hand under the paper, with your other hand moving the paper into position as you cut.

CUTTING WITH A KNIFE

If you are using a knife, work on a cutting board and, whenever possible, move the paper rather than the knife, which should be cutting towards you.

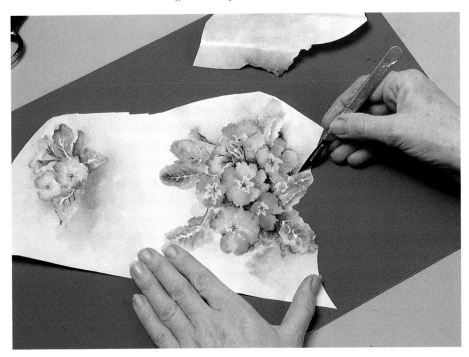

CUTTING WITH SCISSORS

Small scissors are perfect for cutting out the swirling shapes of these flowers, but use the larger ones for cutting the paper into more manageable pieces.

Always cut the small "inner" pieces of background first, leaving the outside contours until near the end. Also, leave any flimsy, delicate pieces well supported by adjacent background until the very last minute.

As you cut each piece, store it carefully where it cannot get lost or creased, until you are ready to plan your design. I keep my cutouts in flat, plastic display pages, so that I can see what they are and check that they are not creased, but putting them between the pages of a book does just as well.

When you are sure that you have cut out enough for your design, arrange the pieces on the article to be decorated and hold them temporarily in place with temporary adhesive. It's a good idea to give some thought to your design at this stage, because you will have already spent a lot of time in the preparation of this piece and you still have more to do. It would be a shame to spoil it all by just plunking the design down anywhere.

Avoid scattering design elements all over the piece in a haphazard manner, for example. Try to give some kind of focal point to the design and tie any other sections to this, using either color or shape.

Above all, if you have a strong feeling that the whole thing would all fall into place if only you had a tree to put here or a few birds to scatter there, go out and find them and then get cutting! You will never be truly happy with the design if you don't.

GLUING

There are two methods of gluing advocated by decoupeurs. One involves spreading small amounts of glue onto the object before laying each design piece into place, and the other is simply to glue the back of the paper cutout before arranging it in its permanent place.

There are advantages and drawbacks to both methods, but on the whole, unless you are creating a very intricate design, I think I prefer the second. I use an old plastic chopping board to glue on so that I can wash it down frequently between pieces, but you can also use pieces of aluminium kitchen foil and throw them away when they get too sticky.

If you are gluing onto a latex surface, a slight spray with sealer (page 12) will make the surface less porous and give you more time to arrange your design. As you glue each piece down, it is important to make sure that it is absolutely smooth and that all the edges are well attached. I usually go over larger cutouts with a rubber roller to squeeze out any air bubbles or deposits of excess glue, and then I clean up any extra glue with a soft cloth, which has previously been wrung out in warm water. Next, I go around the edges of each piece, pressing them down firmly with a glue-free fingertip. (I find it simpler to dispense with the roller for smaller, more fragile cutouts and just use clean fingers and the cloth to smooth them down.) Finally I check, yet again, to see that all the edges are well glued.

▲
8

ARRANGING THE DESIGN

Arrange the paper cutouts on the rod and attach using the temporary adhesive. Remember that the rod has to look good from all sides, so watch out for any trailing pieces that might creep around and turn up where you do not want them.

▲
9

GLUING THE DESIGN

As you glue each piece down, make sure it is absolutely smooth and that all the edges are well attached. I usually go over larger cutouts with a rubber roller to squeeze out any excess glue and then clean up any extra glue with a soft cloth wrung out in warm water.

Should you find a loose edge that has previously missed your eagle eye, take a small amount of glue on the end of a toothpick, and slide it under the paper, holding it down for a second or two with your fingertip.

When you are quite happy that the design is safely glued down, check for any telltale shiny areas of excess glue. If you find any, wash them away carefully with a soft cloth or small piece of sponge wrung out in fairly warm water.

VARNISHING

The aim when varnishing a piece of decoupage is to completely submerge the design, so that if you were to run your finger across the surface of your work, you would not be able to detect the edges of the paper cutouts. As you can imagine, it takes a great many layers of varnish to achieve this state of affairs, but, as I said in the Introduction, it is for you to decide where you wish to stop.

Although drips and runs need to be avoided at all cost, varnish should be applied to the surface in generous strokes before being brushed out lightly across the original brush strokes. With

10
VARNISHING THE DESIGN

Apply two coats of varnish, allowing 24 hours between each. Rub down and wipe with a tack cloth. Apply at least six more coats of varnish, rubbing down and wiping between each. Give one more light rubdown, then wax.

polyurethane varnishes, you need not rub down and wipe until after the second or third coat has dried, and with water-based varnishes you may complete three or four coats before it becomes necessary. After that, though, you must rub down and wipe *very* lightly after every coat.

Don't forget, especially with the early layers, that the vulnerable paper cutouts are only just beneath the surface. If you do happen to catch one with the sandpaper, it will leave a glaring white mark, which you can usually disguise by smudging on some oil-based or watercolor pencils. You will need to seal the repair with a spray of acrylic sealer, but then you can go on varnishing as usual.

WAXING AND ANTIQUING

When you have applied your final coat of varnish, you may well let out a huge sigh of relief and leave it at that, but you can, if you like, go on and give your work an antiqued or waxed surface, or even both. Whichever you choose, you will first need to give the surface a slight roughness by rubbing it down lightly with fine steel wool or sandpaper.

Waxing

Basically, this is just a question of getting a good wax and following the instructions on the container, but you know what they say: To get that really deep sheen you need to wax every day for a week, every week for a month and every month for a year . . . at least! (You can, incidentally, also get quite a passable antiqued finish by applying a tinted wax instead of the usual clear variety.)

Creating a plain antiqued finish

You will need (for a small to medium-sized item) *raw umber artist's oil paint · black artist's oil paint · mineral spirits · jar · artist's paintbrush · 2 small house-painting brushes · some old nylon stockings or tights*

1. Squeeze into the bottom of the jar approximately 1 inch (2.5cm) of raw umber oil paint and about ¼ inch (6mm) of the black. Add a little of the mineral spirits and make a smooth creamy paste with the artist's paintbrush. Gradually add a little more mineral spirits until your mixture is slightly thinner than cream.

2. Using one of the house-painting brushes, paint this mixture over the entire piece, poking it well into any nooks and crannies and especially around locks or handles.

3. Leave the antiquing until it has lost all its gloss but has not dried, and then, with a clean cloth in your free hand, take a clean, dry, house-painting brush and work the antiquing well into the surface while at the same time gradually removing a large portion of it. Keep wiping the brush on the cloth as you work, and stop when your design begins to show through quite clearly.

4. Cut the nylon tights or stockings into medium-sized pieces and form each piece into a wad. Take one of these and begin rubbing the surface in a circular motion.

Your imagination and artistry need to come into play now as you rub more of the antiquing off where the item might have gotten worn over the years, and leave more of it on where dirt might have collected. Changing the nylon wads as they get dirty, continue to work in a circular motion, emphasizing some parts of the design by rubbing off more of the antiquing fluid and leaving other parts more obscure by leaving them fairly dark. When you are quite happy with the effect, leave the antiquing until it is completely dry, then protect it with a coat of varnish.

Creating a "crackle" varnish finish

Sooner or later, everyone wants to have a go at crackle varnish or "craqueleur," as it is sometimes called. I have to admit that you do hear some horror stories about failed attempts to achieve this surface, but if you use the ready-made variety, which is easily available in craft shops now, and follow the instructions *carefully*, you should succeed.

You will usually find two bottles in the packet you buy. The first one is an oil-based, and usually antiqued, varnish, which you paint on first and allow to dry to the point of tackiness. You then paint on the second varnish, which is water-based and fast-drying. The cracks appear on the surface after the second coat has dried because the oil-based coat is still drying.

11

ANTIQUING – RUBBING THE FLUID BACK
When the fluid has dulled, take a clean paintbrush and work it into the wood. Make a wad from a piece of nylon and begin to rub the antiquing off a little, taking more off where there would have been a lot of use.

The best guide is your sense of touch. If you want fairly large cracks, paint on the second coat when the first one is tacky. Test this in an unobtrusive spot, since, if it is about right, it will leave a slight mark. If you want much smaller cracks, allow the first coat to *almost* dry. Reluctant cracks can be encouraged by the use of a hair dryer, but don't hold it too close or have it set too hot, or you might completely ruin the surface.

When everything has dried out, the cracks will need emphasizing; otherwise, they will hardly show, so add a little more of the mineral spirits to the recipe for antiquing (above) and paint this over the whole thing. Leave it for a minute or two until you can see that it is seeping into the cracks, and then wipe off all the excess color with a soft cloth. Allow the final surface to dry thoroughly and finish with a coat of varnish.

Sponging

I have used a sponging technique in two of the projects in this book. On the sewing cabinet (page 63) I used acrylic paints, and on the cart (page 66) I used an oil-based paint glaze and a mixture of gum arabic and bronze powder.

Sponging with Acrylics

The main thing about acrylics is that they dry so quickly. This means that you have to work faster than with other mediums, but it also gives you the advantage of being able to get on with the next stage of your design almost instantly.

You will need (for the sewing cabinet)
1 container of pale yellow acrylic craft paint · small natural sponge · piece of paper · 1 container of pale green acrylic craft paint

1. Put some yellow paint into a saucer and mix it with a little water to a milky consistency.

2. Rinse and wring out the sponge before squeezing it out in some of this mixture. Before you start sponging your item, dab the sponge onto a piece of paper to remove any excess paint. Don't try to get a regular pattern of sponge marks, but twist and turn your sponge so that you get a random overall effect. Add paint to your sponge from time to time.

3. Repeat the same thing with the green paint, making sure that you are leaving some of the yellow and some of the base coat showing through. Always remember to practice on the paper before working directly onto your piece.

If you are working on a big piece, you may find that you will get a buildup of drying paint on your sponge. If this happens, simply rinse it out in warm water and continue.

The yellow will probably be dry before you apply the green, but if you are working on something fairly small and the first coat is still wet, you can still apply the second coat if you wish to get a much softer effect.

Acrylic paint is difficult to remove once it has dried, so make sure that you wash your sponge, saucers and any brushes that you might have used as soon as you have finished.

Sponging with an Oil-Based Paint Glaze

An oil-based glaze doesn't dry as quickly as an acrylic glaze, and in this case we will be sponging off rather than sponging on. If you wish to sponge on a second color, you may do it while the glaze is still wet, but if you wish to sponge on gold as I have done, it is better to let the first coat dry, since it will lose its shine if you allow it to merge with wet paint.

You will need (for the cart)
Ultramarine artist's oil paint · artist's paintbrush · mineral spirits · jar · white oil-based satin paint · white

paper · small house-painting brush · small natural sponge · bronze powder (gold) · gum arabic

1. Take a little of the ultramarine and, using the artist's paintbrush, mix it to a creamy consistency, with a little of the mineral spirits, in the bottom of the jar. Stirring all the time, gradually add the white paint until you think that you have achieved the right shade. Take a little of the paint on an old knife and smear it on a piece of white paper, so that you can see what color it will be when it has been made more transparent by the addition of mineral spirits. Make any necessary adjustments by adding either more white paint or more diluted oil paint. When you are quite happy with the test on paper, stir in slightly less of the mineral spirits than you have paint in the jar.

2. Using the house-painting brush, paint this mixture onto the item to be sponged. If it is a large piece, paint only one part of it at a time, but stop in a logical place so that you don't get a seam when you resume painting.

Take the sponge and, working randomly, dab it all over the painted area, producing a soft cloudy effect. Clean your sponge on a piece of rag from time to time, or rinse it out in mineral spirits and soapy water if you are working on a big piece and get a buildup of paint.

Allow twenty-four hours for the paint to dry and then mix a little of the bronze powder with some gum arabic in an old saucer. Squeeze the sponge out in this mixture and dab it on a piece of paper until it leaves a very light impression. Dab this sparingly among the blue and allow to dry.

VARNISHED GLASS
A piece of varnished glass is a very easy-to-make piece of equipment, which you will find invaluable when you are mixing your own colors for a base coat or trying to work to a specific color scheme.

To make one, you will need a 6- by 4-inch (15 × 10cm) piece of ordinary picture glass and some polyurethane varnish. Leaving a strip at one end to hold it by and making sure that all the brush strokes go in one direction, apply one coat of varnish to the glass. Allow this to dry, then apply a second coat of varnish in the opposite direction. Continue in this way until you have built up at least six coats of varnish.

To use this new tool, simply hold it over any base coats or cutouts that you may be considering for a specific project, and it will instantly give you a good idea of how the colors will look when the project is eventually finished and varnished.

SPONGING OFF

Take the sponge and, working randomly, dab it all over the painted area, producing a soft cloudy effect. Clean your sponge from time to time if you get a buildup of paint.

I love the "transformation scene" that comes at the end of pantomimes when everyone and everything is revealed in all their glory. I had the same kind of feeling when I was painting and decoupaging the old and decrepit pieces in these projects.

If, however, you do not share my penchant for rags to riches, there are plenty of new items to decorate, such as wooden trays and boxes and metal jugs and coal scuttles. These are available in a variety of stores and have the advantage of being easy to find.

Caddy

In England, a caddy used especially to carry garden tools is known as a "trug." I found this lovely old trug, full of tools and covered in oil, at the back of my father's shed. Since he didn't know its origins but thought that it had probably belonged to his father, or possibly even his father's father, I managed to convince him that it was practically an antique and deserved a better fate.

Preparing

You will need:
- Coarse and fine sandpaper
- Acrylic sealer
- Latex paint
- Gold tempera paint

Decorating

You will need:
- Paper cutouts
- Temporary adhesive
- White glue
- Soft cloth and warm water
- Roller
- Clear, satin polyurethane varnish
- Clear, gloss polyurethane varnish
- Varnish brushes

When I had given it a good scrub with bleach to get rid of all the oil, I could see that it was made from pine and that it still had the battered remnants of an ancient coat of flat paint over the usual old red ocher primer. Since people labor for hours or pay good money to achieve this kind of "distressed," or worn, finish, I decided to leave the outside just as it was and simply give the inside two or three coats of flat latex paint, mixed to match the remains of the soft dusty green on the outside.

PREPARING THE CADDY

Since the caddy had been so heavily covered in oil and dirt, it needed a fairly substantial scrub with bleach and detergent. I would not normally recommend this, as it tends to lift the grain, but I was going for the worn look anyway, so I broke the rules.

1 The caddy after being scrubbed with bleach, and looking decidedly worn.

2 After rubbing down the inside of the caddy, I applied the first of three coats of flat latex paint, which was mixed on a special machine in a hardware store, to exactly match the ancient green paint on the outside.

Consequently, it needed a good rubdown with coarse sandpaper before being finished off with fine sandpaper to give it a really smooth surface.

This done, I sealed the outside of the caddy and the handle with an acrylic sealer, so that when I came to apply the design, the wood, which had been left very porous, would not absorb the glue.

The inside was painted with three coats of green latex paint, which was mixed to match the outside at a local hardware store. I rubbed down the latex paint, very lightly, after the second and third coat.

When the latex paint was quite dry, I took some well-stirred, but undiluted gold tempera paint and painted it roughly around the upper rim of the

caddy and along the edges of the handle. I rubbed this into the wood a little with my finger, so that the bare wood showed through in places, matching the worn look of the outside. I then applied more acrylic sealer to the whole thing.

DECORATING THE CADDY

I arranged the design on the caddy and fixed it in place with temporary adhesive. Then I glued the design onto the outside and handle of the caddy.

My angels were so large that I had to bend their halos onto the gold edge of the caddy, where they merged well with the gold paint, although I''m not too sure about the ethics of bending halos!

Because of the size of the paper cutouts, I used the roller to squeeze out any excess glue and wiped it up with the cloth wrung out in warm water.

Even so, I still pressed around the edges once more with a clean fingertip and checked for any pieces that were not stuck down.

I rather liked the look of the dull latex paint that lined the caddy, so I decided to create a contrast by varnishing the inside with satin varnish and the outside with gloss.

Since I had added a butterfly to the inside, it meant that I had to give it just as many coats as the outside; otherwise, I could have gotten away with a couple of coats on the plain latex, instead of the eight that I put all over.

3 When it came to choosing a design for the caddy, I tried to think what other uses it might be put to, besides storing tools, and thought that it might look quite at home in a church, either full of candles or pressed into service by the flower arrangers. These wonderful Byzantine angels with golden halos strike just the right ecclesiastical note.

*H*amper

One of the things I enjoy most about decoupage is the way it can make a silk purse out of a sow's ear. For example, you cannot imagine how battered this hamper was when I first came across it. It was filthy and part of it had actually been burned. With a slight variation on the decoupage theme, however, it has been reincarnated and is now ready to resume life as a knitting basket or newspaper holder. It might even go on a picnic!

Preparing

You will need:

- Oil-based satin paint
- Scissors
- House-painting brush
- Piece of non-fraying fabric
- Temporary adhesive
- White glue
- Soft, lint-free cloth
- Acrylic craft paint
- Artist's paintbrush
- Polyurethane clear gloss varnish

PREPARING AND DECORATING THE HAMPER

1 The hamper was so dirty that it needed scrubbing with hot soapy water before it could be painted. When it was dry, it was given two coats of oil-based satin paint.

2 Using small, sharp scissors, I cut the design elements from the fabric in exactly the same way as when cutting from paper. I then arranged the pieces on the hamper and attached them with temporary adhesive. When I was satisfied with the design, I took one piece at a time and pasted the back generously with glue.

3 Dealing with one piece of fabric at a time, I placed the glued cutout back onto the hamper and pressed it well into the weave with a cloth, which had been wrung out in hot water.

4 I finished by painting the rim and handle with two coats of acrylic paint. When everything was dry, I gave the whole thing at least three coats of polyurethane clear gloss varnish.

Victorian curtain rod and rings

This Victorian curtain rod started life at 7½ feet (2.2m) and was destined to grace the French windows at one end of my living room. It is now just over 6 feet (1.8m) and will luckily make a stunning focal point of my bedroom window. I said "luckily" because herein lies a cautionary tale. Having seen a very old, very beautiful, and very expensive rod at one of those antique shows where I can never afford to buy anything, I decided to obtain the raw material and make my own.

Preparing

You will need:

- New or old curtain rod, approximately 2½ in. (6.5cm) in diameter and complete with end finials and curtain rings
- Wood filler
- Fine sandpaper
- Tack cloth
- Wood primer
- Oil-based satin paint
- House-painting brush
- String
- Mineral spirits (to clean brushes)

Decorating

You will need:

- Largish paper cutouts for the rod and something similar but smaller for the rings
- Sealer, if using the rod unpainted
- White glue
- Soft, lint-free cloth
- Roller
- Polyurethane clear varnish
- Tack cloth
- Very fine sandpaper
- Wax

These old rods are at least 2½ inches (6.5cm) in diameter, and at the time it appeared (falsely) that this size was not available new.

Tracking down an old one with sufficient usable rings was a nightmare, but once I found one, I was not about to let it go . . . even though it was riddled with ancient woodworms! I can't say that I wasn't warned. Everyone who came into the studio mentioned it at least once, but I had been assured that the worms were long gone and I had also treated the rod with a woodworm solution. I

should have known better, but was desperate, so I went ahead and began by drilling the two ¾-inch (2cm) holes at either end for the finials.

The first one was fine, but as I drilled the second one, at least 1 foot (30cm) of the rod dropped off and practically broke my toe! You have been warned.

PREPARING THE CURTAIN ROD AND RINGS

My rod was so old that it had virtually no polish or varnish on it. If yours has and it is intact, you might decide to decoupage directly onto it, but

1 I started with quite a variety—a worm-infested rod, some quite nicely varnished old rings and brand new finials. I think that we can safely assume that your rod will not be infested like mine, but if it is, your first task will be to treat it with a woodworm solution, following the instructions on the container very carefully.

don't forget where it has been—it will probably have years of grease on it, so give it a good wipe with a cloth that has been wrung out in hot soapy water. If it has a cracked or peeling paint or varnish finish on it, this is the time to strip it (see page 16).

If you manage to obtain an old rod, it may have some cracks and blemishes that will need filling. When you use wood filler, don't forget to allow time for it to dry.

I rubbed the rod down gently with fine sandpaper, then wiped it with a tack cloth (see page 19). You will need to do this with any rod that has been stripped or filled—or even with one that is new. I then applied primer, according to the instructions on the container. I left this to dry, then rubbed it down gently and wiped the whole thing. I then applied three or four coats of satin paint,

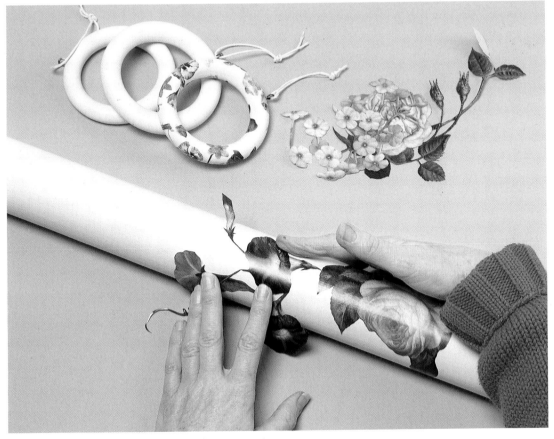

2 My rod needed new finials, and I was lucky enough to find a store that sold the right size, although I had to redrill the holes for them with a special 1-inch (2.5cm) drill. Don't forget, though, that you cannot attach them permanently until everything is finished and the rings are on the rod!

3 I arranged the paper cutouts on the rod and attached them with temporary adhesive. The rod had to look good from all sides, so I had to watch out for any trailing pieces that might creep around and turn up where I didn't want them!

allowing twenty-four hours' drying time between each coat, and rubbed down and wiped between applications. By then I was left with a fine silky finish, which needed just the lightest of rubdowns to give it a slight roughness for the decoupage. I then went over it once again with a tack cloth.

The wooden rings all had little metal rings screwed into the tops of them. I left these in place and threaded a knotted loop of string through each of them, so that they could be suspended while drying. I then treated the rings in the same way as the rod, giving them one extra check for drips after each coat of paint.

DECORATING THE CURTAIN ROD AND RINGS

If the rod is to remain unpainted, seal the rod, rings and finials. Remember also that the rings will need to be decorated on the insides as well as the outsides.

You may arrange the design on the rings so that they match, but since I had at least fourteen, I opted for a more random effect and made it up as I went along. Taking the largest of the design elements first, I applied glue to the back of the paper and fixed it in place on the rod. Since a rod of this size has a generous curve, I didn't have too much trouble keeping a smooth surface.

Keeping my fingertips free of glue, I used them to massage the paper into place, then wiped off any excess glue.

Any tucks in the paper because of the curve can be carefully smoothed out by being pressed alternately with your fingertips and the cloth that has been wrung out in hot water.

If the tucks are really too big to disappear in this way, you may have to ease the paper away from the rod and make a nick in it before carefully gluing it back into position.

With the bigger design elements, it is advisable to run over them with the roller to ensure that any excess glue gets squeezed out and cleaned up with the damp cloth. I continued to fix the design in

place on both the rod and the rings. Having checked again for any unstuck corners, I left it to dry. I then applied two coats of varnish, allowing twenty-four hours between each, rubbed down and wiped.

I applied at least six more coats of varnish, rubbing down and wiping between each.

Finally, I gave one more very light rubdown and waxed the whole thing.

4 To varnish the rings, I applied two coats of varnish, allowing twenty-four hours between each, then rubbed down and wiped. I then applied at least six more coats of varnish, rubbing down and wiping between each. Finally, I gave one more very light rubdown and waxed the surface.

Hatbox

I love hatboxes almost as much as I love hats, but although I've got several of them decorated in various styles, I think that this one is my favorite. It is decorated in the traditional Victorian manner with a multitude of overlapping "scraps," which are little embossed pictures depicting a variety of subjects, from wildlife to the high fashion of Victorian times, when they were first published.

Preparing

You will need:
- Cardboard hatbox base
- Acrylic sealer
- 2–3 sheets of darkish wrapping paper
- Pencil
- Scissors
- Ruler
- White glue
- Soft lint-free cloth
- Roller

Decorating

You will need:
- Several sheets of scraps
- Small curved scissors
- Temporary adhesive
- White glue
- Soft lint-free cloth
- Polyurethane clear varnish
- House-painting brush
- Fine sandpaper
- Tack cloth

Luckily for us, the original scraps are being reproduced again today and are available in craft shops, together with the cardboard bases for the hatboxes.

1 These cardboard hatboxes are a godsend to decoupeurs and collectors alike. They come in at least four sizes and, once decorated, make beautiful containers for all sorts of paraphernalia.

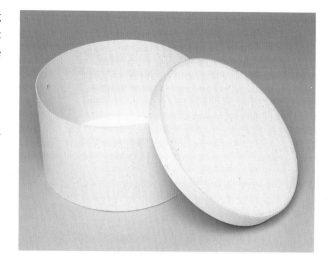

PREPARING THE HATBOX
- Since the hatbox is made from cardboard, it is a good idea to give it a spray with acrylic sealer so that the glue will not be absorbed too quickly when you are sticking on the base paper.
- While the spray is drying, lay the lid of the box upside down on the reverse side of a piece of wrapping paper and draw around it lightly with a pencil.
- Carefully draw a second circle approximately 1 inch (2.5cm) outside the first circle. You will have to do this freehand, so don't worry if it wobbles a bit.
- Cut around the freehand pencil line with scissors, so that you end up with a circle of wrapping paper with a pencil circle drawn 1 inch (2.5cm) in from the outside edge.

- Working around the edge of the circle, cut into the pencil line at intervals of about 1 inch (2.5cm).
- Repeat this process, using the base of the hatbox. Mark the base with a small "b," since the two pieces look very similar in size but are significantly different.
- Measure the length and depth of the circumference of the lid, and cut out a piece of wrapping paper that is the same length but 1 inch (2.5cm) deeper than this.
- Draw a pencil line 1 inch (2.5cm) from the edge of this piece of paper and along the length.
- Working along this edge, cut into the pencil line at approximately 1 inch (2.5cm) intervals.
- Repeat this process to cut a piece of paper to fit the sides of the base of the hatbox, remembering to leave 1 inch (2.5cm) to spare on the depth.

- Paste the back of the circle of paper reserved for the lid with glue, and place it onto the outside of the lid so that the fringed edge is sticking out all around.
- Using a cloth wrung out in warm water, smooth the paper onto the lid, working out from the middle and making sure that there are no pockets of excess glue, creases or air bubbles. Finally, go over it with a roller.
- Check that the underside of the fringed edge is still well covered in glue and then work around the edge of the lid, pressing down every other tab. Repeat with the second set of alternate tabs so that they slightly overlap the first.
- Repeat this process with the second circle to cover the bottom of the hatbox.
- Paste the back of the strip reserved for the edge of the lid, and glue it around the outside of the circumference so that the fringed edge can be bent over and glued inside the lid, using the same method as before.
- Do the same with the strip reserved for the sides of the base, pasting the fringed edge inside the box once more.
- Be especially careful to keep the sides of the box smooth by wiping the paper with the cloth as you fit it around the box.

DECORATING THE HATBOX

Although the scraps are partly cut out, you will still need to trim them and cut out some small background pieces here and there.
- When you have had a good look through your collection and trimmed the scraps, choose a few of the larger ones to make the center piece of your design. Although this type of decoupage looks random, you still need some kind of master plan.
- It isn't practical to tack every scrap onto the hatbox with temporary adhesive before you start gluing, but it is a good idea to fix the major elements in place to remind yourself which pieces you wish to have stand out; otherwise they can get lost underneath a lot of little scraps.

- Once the main elements are held in place with temporary adhesive, you can start gluing your scraps on, making sure that you press each one in place with a cloth wrung out in warm water and checking that all the edges are completely stuck down. (This is the one form of decoupage where it is permissible to allow the scraps to overlap. You will also find that, if you have chosen your base paper wisely, it will not matter if you occasionally leave a *small* gap.)
- When you have completely covered the outside of the box, apply four coats of varnish, allowing twenty-four hours between each application.
- After the fourth coat is dry, sand the whole thing *very* lightly and wipe (see page 19), but remember that with this kind of decoupage you are dealing with an uneven surface. You must therefore be extremely careful not to rub too hard when

2 *I was lucky enough to find a base paper that was actually decorated with Victorian scraps. If you can't find anything similar, any darkish paper will do, provided it has a light-colored reverse side so that you can draw and cut accurately.*

Lining

You will need:
- 2 sheets of wrapping paper
- Pencil
- Scissors
- Ruler
- White glue
- Soft lint-free cloth
- Acrylic sealer
- Satin varnish

3 *Scraps usually come partly cut out, in sheet form, and will still need a little trimming.*

sanding, or you will catch the scraps and ruin them. If you do have a mishap of this kind, try to repair the damage with oil-based colored pencils softened into the original print with the tip of your finger. Fix the repair with sealer and continue varnishing, but don't forget that this particular spot will be very vulnerable every time you sand.

● It is up to you how many coats of varnish you apply, but ideally you should not be able to feel the edges of the scraps when you have finished. This will take at least twenty more coats of varnish with sanding and wiping in between.

I know that the temptation to stop after a few more coats is very strong, but patience is a virtue and if you do press on, your reward will be the awesome sight of the scraps glowing deeply from beneath layers and layers of mellow varnish.

LINING THE HATBOX

● Place the lid and the base on the wrong side of the wrapping paper and draw around both.
● Cut out the circles and mark them lightly so that you know which is which.
● Cut out two strips for the sides of the base and lid, following the instructions for the outside.
● Fold the fringed edge of the base strip back towards the right side of the paper and crease well.
● Straighten out the paper and apply a good coat of glue before fitting the strip inside the base, so that the fringed edge is bent and pasted onto the bottom of the box. Use the same technique for fixing the fringe as before, and smooth everything into place with a cloth wrung out in warm water.
● Line the side of the lid in the same way.
● Paste the base circle and glue it into the bottom

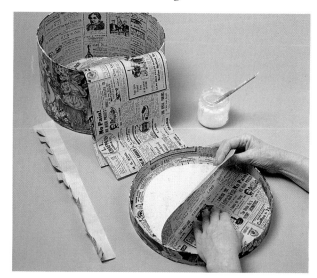

4 *This ancient newspaper, which gives such an air of authenticity to my Victorian hatbox, is actually a piece of modern wrapping paper. If you can not find paper like this, choose a paper in a neutral color and with a small pattern.*

BOW

You will need:

- 3ft. (1m) white curtain lining material
- Scissors
- Dressmaker's pins
- White cotton
- White glue or fabric stiffener
- 2 plastic bags
- 1 bottle of poppy red acrylic craft paint
- Brush
- Varnish

of the box so that it completely covers the fringed edge of the sides, and smooth with the cloth as you did for the lid.

- Glue the lid circle into place in the same way.
- When everything has dried out, apply one coat of sealer followed by one coat of satin varnish.

MAKING THE STIFFENED BOW

The cardboard hatboxes come in a variety of sizes, so you will have to judge exactly how large to make your bow. My box measured 1 foot (30cm) in diameter. For one the same size, follow these instructions:

- Cut out three pieces of material: two pieces measuring 24 by 10 inches (60 × 25cm), and one piece measuring 18 by 10 inches (45 × 25cm).
- Fold them all in half lengthwise and mark a point halfway along the unfolded length of each of them with a pin.
- Take one of the larger pieces and machine-stitch along one end to within 2 inches (5cm) of the pin along the length. Repeat this at the other end so that you have a 4-inch (10cm) gap in the middle of the unfolded long side. Use this to turn the strip inside

Trim off the excess material so that the strip has a tail at either end.

out, before slip-stitching the gap together.

- Smooth the strip flat with your hands and mark a point halfway along the length with a pin. Fold both ends toward the middle so that they butt together at this point. Machine-stitch ends in place so that you have a loop of material at either end.
- Repeat this process with the shorter strip, and then lay the shorter bow on top of the longer one with their smooth sides facing outward.
- Take the other long strip and start your machine-stitching 2 inches (5cm) from the middle pin. Sew straight for about 2 inches (5cm), and then begin to curve your stitching gradually, aiming for the far corner of the strip.
- Treat the other side in the same way, so that you again have a 4-inch (10cm) gap in the middle. Trim off the excess material so that your strip has a tail at either end. Turn the strip in the right way and sew up the gap.
- Knot the tapered strip tightly around the double bow so that it covers the central stitching.

STIFFENING THE BOW

- *If you are using fabric stiffener*, use it according to instructions, although if it has to be diluted, use a little less water than suggested. *If you are using glue*, dilute it with warm water, using one part glue to four parts water.
- Immerse the bow completely in the solution and wring it out thoroughly before arranging it carefully on a board.
- Cut the plastic bags into three or four pieces and use these to stuff the loops of the bows until they are dry. If you are feeling really artistic, you can ruffle up or pleat the tails a little, too. Try not to be too neat with your bow—they look better when they look natural.
- When the bow is completely dry, remove it from the board and give it two coats of acrylic paint.
- When this is dry, give it another two coats of varnish before gluing it onto your hatbox.

Enamel pitcher

Considering their lowly origins, I always think these types of pitchers have incredibly elegant lines, which show up even more when they are decorated. I painted this one with a particularly dull-looking blue, which positively cried out for something exciting to happen to it—before I found these exuberant anemones to cheer it up.

Preparing

You will need:

- Brushes
- Bare metal primer (red oxide)
- Fine sandpaper
- Latex paint
- Tack cloth
- Acrylic sealer

Decorating

You will need:

- Paper cutouts
- Temporary adhesive
- White glue
- Soft lint-free cloth
- Roller
- Acrylic craft paint
- Brushes
- Polyurethane varnish
- Fine sandpaper
- Tack cloth
- Wax

The flowers were actually too big to fit onto the handle, so I painted a thin magenta line on it and pulled the whole design together by using the same color around the top. I also used the butterflies to unify the rather rambling effect of the flowers.

1 I don't know whether you can still buy this sort of pitcher new, but this one turned up in an antique market with a bad case of rust, which had to be dealt with before anything else could happen to it (page 18).

2 When you first start rubbing with fine steel wool and a rust remover, you won't believe that it is possible to remove all the rust and get down to shining metal. Five minutes later, you still won't believe it, if it is a bad case, but you can . . . and you must!

3 The pitcher was painted with two coats of red oxide, inside and out, and when this was dry, it was lightly rubbed down and wiped, before being given several coats of thinned-down latex paint (page 11), followed by a coat of acrylic sealer.

DECORATING THE PITCHER

I arranged the design on the pitcher, using temporary adhesive to hold it in place, and made sure that any trailing ends didn't end up interfering with any other part of the design as they wound around the pitcher. The butterflies were put on last and were placed so that they would add balance to an otherwise rambling design.

When I was happy with the overall design, I took each piece in turn and glued it back in place, wiping it with the cloth initially. Then, because most of the pieces were large, I went over the design again with the roller to squeeze out any excess glue.

When everything was glued in place, I went over the whole thing again, checking all the edges with a fingertip and wiping with a cloth wrung out in warm water.

The handle had been left undecorated and looked a bit out of place until I painted a magenta line down the middle of it. I chose the color to go with the anemones, and I made the line the same width as the curled edge around the rim of the pitcher, which I painted with the same color.

When everything was completely dry, I applied two coats of polyurethane varnish, allowing twenty-four hours between each coat. I then rubbed down the pitcher *very* gently with fine sandpaper and went over it with the tack cloth. I gave the pitcher six more coats of varnish, rubbing down and wiping (see page 19) between each coat. Finally, I waxed it (see page 24).

4 Small scissors are perfect for cutting out the swirling shapes of these flowers, but use the larger ones for dividing the paper into more manageable pieces.

Desk

When I decided that I would like to decoupage a small desk, I went out and looked for an interesting secondhand one in all the local junk and thrift shops. After many fruitless weeks of searching, however, I began to realize that it was impossible to find a desk of any kind, which explains why I jumped at this desk when it turned up, in true savior style, at the back of somebody's stable.

Preparing
You will need:
- Wood filler
- Medium sandpaper
- Fine sandpaper
- Tack cloth
- Water-based undercoat
- Cream latex paint
- Brushes
- Sealer

Decorating
You will need:
- Paper cutouts
- Temporary adhesive
- White glue
- Roller
- Soft lint-free cloth
- Acrylic varnish
- Fine sandpaper
- Tack cloth
- Crackle varnish
- Spar varnish

I have to admit, it was not my idea of a dream desk. It was ugly, it smelled strongly of horses and it was so large that I had to break it down into pieces just to get it through the front door, but it was a desk. I've never worked on anything that provided a greater challenge to the art of decoupage, but now that it's finished I'm really quite fond of it.

PREPARING THE DESK
Since I had spent so much time actually finding the desk, I decided to try to cut down on the drying times by using all water-based materials, but first

I washed the whole thing with hot soapy water (page 17) to get rid of its distinctly equine fragrance! When it was dry, I went over it again, filling in any holes and cracks with wood filler. I allowed this to dry before rubbing everything down, first with medium sandpaper and then with fine, and following with a good dusting with the tack cloth (see page 19).

Before applying the latex paint, I gave the desk two coats of a water-based undercoat and allowed these to dry for the recommended time. I then applied eight thinned-down coats of latex

1 Since I had spent so much time actually finding the desk, I decided to try to cut down on the drying times by using all water-based materials, but first I washed the whole thing with hot soapy water (page 17) to get rid of its distinctly equine fragrance!

paint (see page 19), rubbing down lightly and wiping after the third and every subsequent coat. When I had achieved a smooth, silky finish, I gave the whole desk a coat of sealer.

DECORATING THE DESK

I arranged the paper cutouts so that the design looked well-balanced from any angle, and fixed the pieces temporarily in place with temporary adhesive. When I was quite happy with the design, I removed the pieces one by one and pasted the back of each piece with glue before returning it to its former position. I then went over the desk with the roller to squeeze out any excess glue, which I cleaned up with a soft, damp cloth. When everything was glued in place, I double-checked the edges of each piece and reglued any that had lifted (see page 23).

I allowed the cutouts to dry and then checked for any shiny patches of dried glue that might be still showing. I cleaned these off carefully with a cloth wrung out in warm water and allowed a little time for everything to dry again.

I then applied three coats of acrylic varnish, allowing the recommended drying time between coats. When the last one was quite dry, I *very* gently rubbed the desk down with fine sandpaper before going over it with a tack cloth (see page 19).

I continued applying coats of acrylic varnish, rubbing down and wiping until the edges of the design were completely undetectable.

I decided that the design called for an antique look and gave the desk the two coats required for a crackle finish (see page 25). Finally, I gave it two coats of spar varnish, rubbing down and wiping between the two.

2 When it was dry, I went over it again, filling in any holes and cracks with wood filler, which I allowed to dry before rubbing everything down.

3 I rubbed everything down, first with medium sandpaper and then with fine, then followed up with a good dusting with the tack cloth (page 19).

4 Before applying the latex paint, I gave the desk two coats of a water-based undercoat and allowed these to dry for the recommended time. I then applied eight thinned-down coats of latex paint (page 19), rubbing down lightly and wiping after the third and every subsequent coat. When I had achieved a smooth, silky finish, I gave the whole desk a coat of sealer.

Mirror

Butterflies, bugs and birds are so useful for balancing designs or tying elements together that I seldom make a design without one or the other. It was like that with this mirror, which I decided to decorate for use in a nursery, mainly because I had been longing to use these gorgeous Lawson Wood illustrations.

Preparing

You will need:

- Wood filler
- Medium and fine sandpaper
- Tack cloth
- Wooden knob for the drawer
- Wood glue
- Wood primer
- Oil-based satin paint
- Brushes
- Mineral spirits (to thin brushes)

Decorating

You will need:

- Paper cutouts
- Temporary adhesive
- White glue
- Soft lint-free cloth
- Roller
- Polyurethane clear varnish
- Brushes
- Antiquing materials (page 24)
- Wax

It didn't matter how I put the pictures onto the frame, however; the design always seemed to lack unity. Then I found the little butterflies, which were small and dark and didn't detract from the illustrations, but whose wandering presence tied the whole thing together.

PREPARING THE MIRROR

There was a thick coat of badly applied paint on the mirror when I bought it, which I had stripped off commercially. The stripping revealed all sorts of cracks and holes that had previously been plugged up with paint and that needed filling with wood filler.

Once the filler had dried, the whole thing needed rubbing down, first with medium sandpaper and then with fine. It was then wiped with a tack cloth.

I also fitted a new wooden knob to the drawer at this point, which necessitated drilling a hole before gluing the knob into place. Taking care to rub down and wipe between each coat, I then gave the mirror two coats of primer followed by three coats of paint, allowing twenty-four hours between each application.

DECORATING THE MIRROR

I arranged and rearranged the paper cutouts on the mirror frame with temporary adhesive, until I was happy with the design. I then removed each piece singly, pasted it with glue and returned it to its place. The small pieces I pressed into place with a clean fingertip and a cloth wrung out in warm water,

1 There was a thick coat of badly applied paint on the mirror when I bought it, which I had stripped off commercially.

but I went over the larger ones with the roller to squeeze out any excess glue.

When everything was dry, I double-checked for any loose corners or spots of dried glue, which I reglued or wiped off with the warm damp cloth.

I then gave the whole thing eight coats of varnish, rubbing down and wiping very lightly after every coat except the first one.

When the last coat of varnish was dry, I antiqued (see page 24) the mirror and left it to dry for a few days before giving it a final coat of varnish, followed the next day by an application of wax (see page 24).

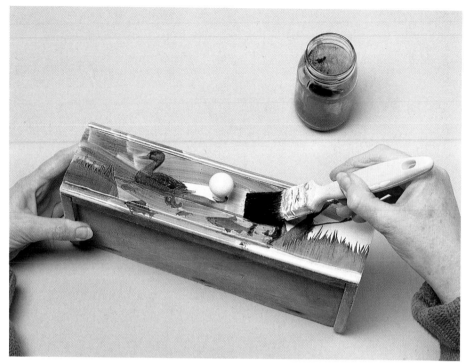

3 To achieve an antiqued look, I painted on a generous coating of antiquing fluid, making sure to push it into all the nooks and crannies. I then left it until it began to dull.

2 The stripping revealed all sorts of cracks and holes that had previously been plugged up with paint, and I filled these with wood filler.

4 When the fluid had dulled, I took a clean paintbrush and worked it into the wood, especially where any dirt would have gathered over the years. Finally, I made a smooth ball from a piece of nylon and began to rub the antiquing off a little, taking more off in places where there would have been a lot of wear—around the drawer knob, for example.

*T*hree-tiered stand

Sunday tea will develop a certain kind of style if you can find one of these old cake stands to decoupage. This one was painted white when I found it, but stripping revealed a layer of orange lacquer, which was so evocative of the 1930s, when it would have been in regular use, that I could not wait to decorate it and get out the china teacups.

Preparing
You will need:
- Stripping materials (page 11)
- Water-based undercoat
- Medium and fine sandpaper
- Tack cloth
- Black latex paint
- Acrylic sealer
- Brushes

Decorating
You will need:
- Paper cutouts
- Temporary adhesive
- White glue
- Roller
- Soft line-free cloth
- Acrylic varnish
- Tack cloth
- Spar varnish
- Wax

Old cake stands are not so difficult to find, but I must warn you, they do exude a certain sort of charm. Before you know it, you could well be serving tiny cucumber sandwiches on lace doilies.

PREPARING THE STAND
After the stand had been stripped (page 16), it was rubbed down thoroughly with both medium and fine sandpapers. However, the stripping had made the wood very "thirsty," and it needed a couple of coats of water-based undercoat before being rubbed down lightly again with the fine sandpaper and wiped. I then gave it two coats of black latex paint and rubbed it down very lightly again, before giving it one final application of latex followed by a coat of sealer.

DECORATING THE STAND
I arranged the cutouts on the stand and fixed them in place with temporary adhesive. When I was quite happy with the overall effect, I removed them one

1 This 1930s cake stand was pretty battered when I bought it, but even then it betrayed a certain style.

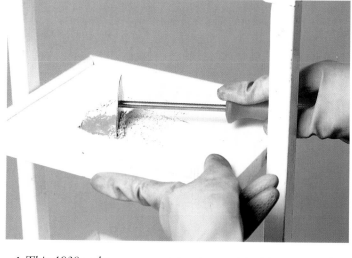

2 After the stand had been stripped (page 16), it had to be rubbed down thoroughly with both medium- and fine-grade sandpapers.

However, the stripping had made the wood very "thirsty," and it needed a couple of coats of water-based undercoat before being rubbed down with fine sandpaper.

by one, pasted them with glue and returned them to their places in the design.

Since they were all rather large pieces, I went over each of them with the roller to squeeze out any excess glue. I then went over the whole thing with a cloth wrung out in warm water, removing any stray glue and checking that all the edges were firmly glued down.

When the design had completely dried out, I gave the stand three or four coats of acrylic varnish, rubbing down the last one *very* gently when dry. I then went over the whole thing with a tack cloth before continuing to add varnish, rub down and wipe until the design was submerged.

Once the last coat was dry, I gave it a light rubdown before applying a coat of spar varnish. Finally, I gave the whole thing a good coat of wax and polished it until it glowed.

4 I waxed this thoroughly after the last application of varnish. To get a really deep glow, wax it again once in a while.

3 Since they were all rather large pieces, I went over each of them with the roller to squeeze out any excess glue. I then went over the whole thing with a warm, damp cloth, removing any stray glue and checking that all the edges were firmly glued down.

Doll's cradle

I pity the poor old doll who slept in this cradle. When I bought it, it was painted heavily with the ugliest pink paint and was absolutely bristling with round-headed screws.

I was so eager to get rid of the awful pink paint that I took it to a commercial stripper on my way home from buying it. Imagine my horror when I returned some days later, only to find that the paint had been of the old and tenacious "nursery" variety, which was never actually *meant* to come off . . . ever!

Preparing

You will need:

- Coarse sandpaper
- Wood filler
- Fine sandpaper
- Tack cloth
- Wood primer
- Brushes
- White oil-based satin paint
- White paper
- Mineral spirits (to clean brushes)
- Artist's oil paints (Ultramarine and Raw Umber)
- Small rectangular piece of varnished glass

Decorating

You will need:

- Paper cutouts
- Temporary adhesive
- White glue
- Roller
- Soft lint-free cloth
- Polyurethane clear varnish
- Brushes

The stripper had done his best, but there still remained a thin layer of the dreaded color, which I rubbed down and covered up as soon as I possibly could.

When I had dealt with the screws and repainted it, the cradle had such a pretty old-fashioned shape that I found that modern pictures just didn't look right on it, while drawings of Edwardian children playing in the park seemed to suit it exactly.

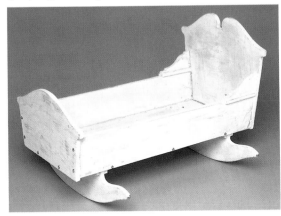

2 To make this soft lavender blue, I mixed about 1 inch (2.5cm) of ultramarine artist's oil paint and just a touch of raw umber with enough mineral spirits to make a creamy consistency. I then gradually added the white satin paint until I arrived at the correct color.

PREPARING THE DOLL'S CRADLE

When something has been stripped as rigorously as this has, you will find that the grain of the wood will be slightly lifted (more so if you have used the caustic method [see page 17]). You might therefore have to rub the piece down a little with coarse sandpaper to see where it needs filling.

I did this, then filled all holes, cracks and

1 Believe it or not, there were thirty-six round-headed screws poking out of this one little doll's cradle when I bought it. These all had to be removed and replaced with flat-headed screws, and the holes filled and rubbed down before anything else could be done.

abrasions with wood filler and let it dry. I then rubbed it down with fine sandpaper until the cradle was smooth, and wiped it with a tack cloth (see page 19). I then applied primer according to the instructions on the container and allowed it to dry, before rubbing it down lightly and wiping.

I then mixed up the color for the base coat (page 19) and smeared a little of the mixed color on a piece of white paper. I viewed the result through a piece of varnished glass (page 27), and made any necessary adjustments. I used this base color to apply three or four coats to the cradle, remembering to rub down and wipe between each application. I waited twenty-four hours between coats (don't be tempted to go any faster, as you have already added extra oil to the mixture, which will slow the drying time) before applying the design. I then rubbed it down very lightly to give a slight roughness and wiped the whole thing.

DECORATING THE DOLL'S CRADLE

I arranged the design on the cradle, using temporary adhesive to hold it in place. I then glued the design in position, using my fingers and the roller to squeeze any excess glue out from under the paper. I then wiped off any extra glue with the soft cloth wrung out in warm water.

I checked that each piece was well glued before going on to the next, by pressing firmly around the edges with the tip of my finger.

When I had completed the design, I reglued loose ends with a little glue on a toothpick.

Before varnishing, I checked for any shiny patches of dried, excess glue and wiped them off with a cloth wrung out in hot water.

I then applied two coats of polyurethane clear varnish, allowing twenty-four hours between each application. After that I rubbed down gently, taking care not to scuff the design.

I went over the cradle once more with the tack cloth and continued to varnish, rub down and wipe until I had sunk the edges of the design.

3 When you are using so many layers of polyurethane varnish, it is inevitable that the original colors will yellow. This is not always a bad thing, since it can have a harmonizing effect, but since you are mixing your own color for this project, you can, as I did, look through the varnished glass and make adjustments.

4 Once you have begun to varnish, anything that is not really glued down will become a problem, so get used to checking and then double-checking!

Cupboard

This chunky old cupboard didn't have a lot going for it when I bought it, except that it represented potential storage space in any one of a umber of rooms. I had originally planned to use it for storing toys, but after new wooden handles and two or three coats of cream paint, it seemed destined for a higher purpose, and I found myself giving in and decorating it with these beautiful classical garlands of roses. After that, it simply had to have an antique finish, and I'll bet that it ends up in the dining room!

Preparing
You will need:
- Mineral spirits
- Fine steel wool
- Wood filler
- Wood primer
- Fine sandpaper
- Tack cloth
- Cream oil-based satin paint
- Brushes

Decorating
You will need:
- Paper cutouts
- Temporary adhesive
- White glue
- Roller
- Soft lint-free cloth
- Polyurethane clear varnish
- Crackle varnish and other antiquing materials (page 24)
- Brushes
- Wax

1 Although the cupboard was plain and chunky and had awful handles, it did have a flawless finish and only needed rubbing down with fine steel wool and mineral spirits to remove grease and dirt.

2 I filled the holes where the old handles had been and painted the new wooden ones with two coats of wood primer. I then rubbed the whole thing down with fine sandpaper and finally went over it completely with a tack cloth (see page 19).

PREPARING THE CUPBOARD
Apart from the holes where the original handles had been, the cupboard had a flawless finish and needed only a rubdown with mineral spirits and fine steel wool to remove any grease and dirt.

I filled the holes with wood filler, which I rubbed down when it was dry, and gave the new wooden handles two coats of wood primer.

I then rubbed the whole thing down lightly with fine sandpaper and went over it with the tack cloth (see page 19). Finally, I gave it three coats of satin paint and rubbed down and wiped between each one.

3 I cut out a design of old-style roses and arranged them in garlands on the cupboard with temporary adhesive.

4 When I was sure that there were no air bubbles or creases, I checked that all the edges were secure before cleaning up the excess glue with a warm, damp cloth.

DECORATING THE CUPBOARD

I arranged the paper cutouts on the cupboard, holding them temporarily with temporary adhesive and making sure that the design looked good from any angle.

I then removed the pieces one by one and pasted them with glue before returning them to their original position.

After gluing each piece in place, I went over the desk with the roller and cleaned up any excess glue with a cloth wrung out in warm water.

When the design was finished, I gave the cupboard two coats of varnish, which I rubbed down lightly after the second one was dry.

I then went over the whole thing with a tack cloth and continued to varnish, rub down and wipe until the design was completely submerged.

I finished off by antiquing the cupboard with crackle varnish (see page 25). When this was dry, I covered it with one coat of polyurethane varnish and waxed it (page 24).

Sewing cabinet

The only thing that was really wrong with this cabinet when I bought it was that it had a split leg, which was easily repaired with wood glue (see page 11). Apart from that, it was perfect for decoupage, since it had so many interestingly shaped surfaces, which were all framed by the main structure of the piece. It was going into a pastel-colored room, so this watercolor design of primulas suited it beautifully.

Preparing

You will need:

- Fine steel wool
- Mineral spirits
- Fine sandpaper
- Tack cloth
- Oil-based satin paint
- Brushes
- Green and yellow acrylic paint and sponging materials (pages 26–27)

Decorating

You will need:

- Paper cutouts
- Temporary adhesive
- White glue
- Damp cloth
- Acrylic varnish
- Brushes
- Tack cloth
- Polyurethane clear gloss varnish
- Fine sandpaper

1 I liked the fact that this cabinet had so many enclosed panels on which to arrange the design, but I decided to change the metal handles to wooden ones, so that they could be painted and become part of the overall scheme.

2 I then used a sanding block, with sandpaper wrapped around it to rub it down. Always sand with the grain, getting your whole arm and shoulder behind the movement instead of just your wrist.

PREPARING THE CABINET

The first thing I did was to go over the whole piece with some fine steel wool and some mineral spirits, to remove any polish and dirt that might be on it. I then rubbed it down with fine sandpaper and went over it with a tack cloth (see page 19).

Because this is a piece of furniture that is likely to get a lot of use, I decided to paint it with an oil-based paint. I gave it five thinned-down coats (see page 11), rubbing down and wiping after the second and each subsequent coat.

The cabinet seemed to lack form once it was painted and looked much better after I had sponged the frame and the edge of the lid (see page 26).

Decorating the Cabinet

I arranged the cutouts onto the box with temporary adhesive and when I was satisfied, I removed the pieces one by one and glued them back in position. Since they were so small, I pressed them into place with a clean fingertip and the damp cloth.

After I had double-checked for any loose corners and stray glue, I gave the cabinet two or three coats of acrylic varnish before rubbing it down lightly.

I then went over it with a tack cloth (see page 19) and continued to varnish, rub down and wipe until the design was completely submerged.

I waited twenty-four hours before giving it a final coat of polyurethane clear gloss varnish.

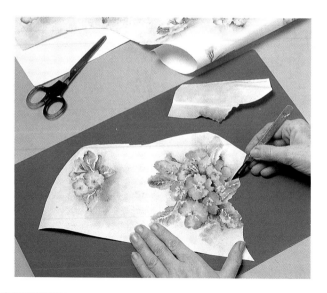

3 *Since this design had a lot of straight-edged leaves and stems, I decided to use a cutting board and knife, using the large scissors to cut the design into manageable pieces.*

4 *I spent hours arranging and re-arranging this design with temporary adhesive and finally made it work by adding some butterflies and dragonflies.*

Cart

This cart is an indulgence on my part, because I have to ration myself where cherubs are concerned. Some people have a weakness for cats or ducks or even pigs, but my inclination is for cherubs, and I could easily put them on almost anything. They look quite at home floating about on the blue-sponged tiers of this cart—I couldn't resist sponging a little gold among the blue either, just to make the whole thing more ethereal.

Preparing

You will need:
- Medium and fine sandpaper
- Tack cloth
- Wood primer
- White oil-based satin paint
- Brushes
- Mineral spirits (to clean brushes)
- Jar
- Blue glaze (pages 26–27)
- Piece of natural sponge
- Gum arabic and gold/ bronze powder *or* gold acrylic paint

Decorating

You will need:
- Acrylic sealer
- Paper cutouts
- Temporary adhesive
- White glue
- Roller
- Soft lint-free cloth
- Acrylic varnish
- Fine sandpaper
- Tack cloth
- Spar varnish

PREPARING THE CART

The cart had such a collection of badly applied coats of paint on it that I had it professionally stripped before removing its rusting hinges (it is collapsible and had 16!) and rubbing it down, first with medium- and then with fine-grade sandpaper.

I then went over it with a tack cloth and gave it two coats of primer and three coats of white paint, allowing the recommended time between applications, in addition to rubbing down and wiping.

When the base coat was completely dry, I painted each piece with a blue glaze (see pages 26–27) and sponged off with a small piece of natural sponge (see page 26).

I allowed the glaze twenty-four hours to dry before giving the trays a *very light* sponging with gold (see page 27).

1 The cart had so many badly applied coats of paint that it went to a commercial stripper before its wheels could touch the ground. It returned revealing sixteen very rusty hinges, which had to be removed and ultimately replaced with new brass ones.

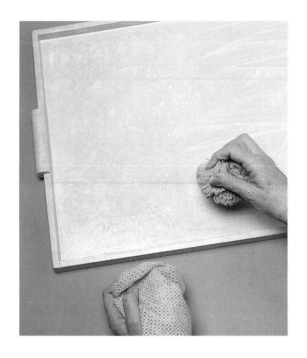

2 The blue glaze was first painted on and then sponged off, using a piece of natural sponge rather than a synthetic one, which gives too uniform a pattern to the sponging.

3 I used a mixture of bronze powder and gum arabic to lightly sponge a little gold onto the cloudy blue background, but you could also use some thinned-down gold acrylic paint if you prefer. The acrylic will dry almost instantly, but will not be quite so brilliantly gold as the bronze powder.

DECORATING THE CART

Before arranging the design, I gave the trays a coating of acrylic sealer to take care of any stray gold that might be floating around. I then arranged the cutouts on the cart with temporary adhesive until I was quite happy with the design from all sides.

After that, I removed each piece singly and pasted the back with glue before returning it to its place.

The larger pieces I went over with the roller to squeeze out any excess glue and creases, but the smaller ones could be satisfactorily smoothed with a clean, glue-free fingertip.

Finally, I checked all the edges to make sure that everything was well glued and went over the design with a cloth wrung out in warm water, to wipe up any excess glue.

When the design had dried out, I gave the cart two or three coats of acrylic varnish, after which I rubbed down *very* lightly and went over the whole thing with the tack cloth (see page 19).

I continued adding coats of varnish, rubbing down gently and wiping until the design was completely submerged. I then gave everything a coat of spar varnish.

4 The center piece and some of the bigger cherubs needed to be smoothed over with a roller, but for the smaller design elements there was no substitute for a glue-free fingertip. Finally, any excess glue was wiped up with a warm, damp cloth.

Silver chest

These old silver chests turn up everywhere, usually with no insides and with their veneers chipped and peeling. This one was no exception, but as I simply cannot resist a lost cause, I decided to give it the works, complete with mother-of-pearl insets and a silk lining. The colors in the mother-of-pearl look really mouthwatering against the black background. They also complement the faded Victorian flower design, which I have allowed to tumble over the edges of the chest to soften its rather hard lines.

Preparing

You will need:
- Palette knife
- Wood glue
- Wood filler
- Fine sandpaper
- Tack cloth
- Black latex paint
- Brushes

Decorating

You will need:
- Paper cutouts
- Temporary adhesive
- Drawing paper and pencil
- Thin mother-of-pearl strips
- Small sharp scissors
- White chalk
- White glue
- Soft lint-free cloth
- Cotton swabs
- Acrylic sealer
- Black latex paint
- Polyurethane varnish
- Fine steel wool
- Mineral spirits

PREPARING THE CHEST

When I inherited this chest, someone had already been at it with varnish stripper, which probably accounted for the state it was in.

I had to stick down the veneer by inserting a palette knife covered in wood glue between it and the body of the chest. I stood an old flat iron on this while it was drying, but any heavy object would have done.

I then filled a multitude of little holes and chips with wood filler, which I rubbed down with fine sandpaper when it was dry, together with the rest of the chest.

After going over the chest with a tack cloth (page 19) I gave it six coats of slightly thinned-down latex paint, lightly rubbing down and wiping every coat except the first.

DECORATING THE CHEST

I arranged my paper cutouts on the chest and held them in place initially with temporary adhesive.

When I was quite happy with the design, I made a rough drawing of the chest and the positions of the design pieces on it. I then soaked the pieces of mother-of-pearl in very hot water so that they would be less brittle when I went to cut them.

I wanted to replace some of the paper details, such as leaves, flower petals and butterflies' wings, with mother-of-pearl, so I removed each design piece from the chest, cut off the part I wanted to

replace, and then returned the remainder to the appropriate position on the chest.

Using the small pieces I had cut off as templates, I laid each one on a piece of softened mother-of-pearl and cut around the shape with the scissors. I then stuck the replacement piece of mother-of-pearl back onto the design with temporary adhesive.

When I had replaced all the pieces I wanted with

1 *After I had glued down the veneer and filled all the chips and holes, the chest was rubbed down and given six coats of slightly thinned-down latex paint (see page 11).*

2When I had arranged the design to my satisfaction, I held it temporarily in place with temporary adhesive and made a rough drawing of the box so that I could relocate the pieces later on, when the mother-of-pearl was in place.

mother-of-pearl, I removed all the paper pieces and wrote a different letter on the back of each and on the corresponding part of the drawing.

The mother-of-pearl pieces still remained on the chest, and I drew around each one with a piece of chalk before removing them one by one, gluing their backs and returning them to their places. I pressed each one down firmly with a clean fingertip and wiped off any excess glue and the chalk marks with a cloth wrung out in warm water. I then left them for several hours to dry thoroughly.

When the glue had completely dried, I gave the chest another coat of black latex paint, removing it quickly from the mother-of-pearl with a cotton swab rinsed in warm water.

I gave the chest a coat of sealer when the paint was dry, being careful, once more, to remove any traces of it from the mother-of-pearl with a damp cotton swab.

The chest was now ready to glue the paper designs on so that they fitted around the mother-of-pearl in the correct way. This I did with the help of my drawing.

Finally, I gave the chest six coats of varnish, rubbing down and wiping very carefully from the third coat onward with a piece of fine steel wool. After each coat, I carefully removed any that had landed on the mother-of-pearl with a cotton swab dipped in mineral spirits.

I then put on one last coat of varnish, this time over the entire surface of the chest, mother-of-pearl and all.

3Mother-of-pearl is very brittle and needs to be soaked in hot water for a minute or two, to be softened before you cut it. It cools quickly, though, so I had to keep putting it back in the hot water as I worked.

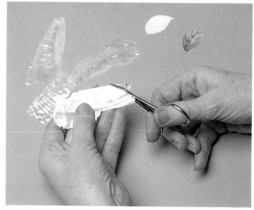

4Latex paint dries fairly quickly, so I removed it from the mother-of-pearl with a cotton swab rinsed in warm water as soon as I could.

*P*otichomanie glass jar

If that sounds like rather a grand name for a jar that you may well end up keeping your bath salts in, then let me tell you that "potichomanie" is a traditional variation of decoupage that goes back to the second half of the last century, and some say even earlier than that.

I have chosen this particular jar because it is a type that is widely available and because you can easily get your hand inside it. However, if you have small hands and a lot of patience, you could try one of the more elegant glass vases that were so much in vogue in the nineteenth century.

For a totally authentic look, you could decorate it with antique Oriental figures, but if these proved difficult to find, Victorian scraps (see page 10) would do as well.

Decorating

You will need:

- Small paper cutouts
- Temporary adhesive
- White glue
- Small piece of sponge
- Oil-based satin paint
- Medium-sized artist's sable brush
- Mineral spirits (to clean brushes)

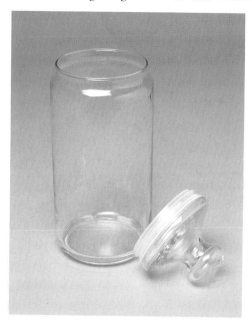

1 I chose a jar that was large enough to get my hand inside, and made sure that the inside was well polished and completely free of dust or grease.

2 I arranged my paper cutouts on the outside of the jar, using temporary adhesive to hold them in place.

4 When the jar was completely dry, I painted the inside, using the sable brush and working in short strokes, spiraling from the bottom. I painted over the paper cutouts so that the brush only moved outward over the edges. I used the paint sparingly so that there was no risk of it dribbling down the sides. I then left the first coat to dry for 24 hours, before applying the second.

3 When I was quite happy with the design, I removed the cutouts in turn and pasted the right side of each with glue, before restoring them to the same position, but this time I stuck them onto the inside of the glass. I then pressed each piece firmly into place with my fingertips, making sure that all the edges were completely glued.

DECORATING THE JAR

I made sure that the inside of the jar was dust- and grease-free by polishing it with a soft cloth. I then arranged the paper cutouts on the outside of the jar, using temporary adhesive to hold them in place.

When I was quite happy with the design, I removed the cutouts in turn and pasted the *right* side of each with glue, before restoring them to the same position, only this time I stuck them onto the *inside* of the glass. I then pressed each piece firmly into place with my fingertips, making sure that all the edges were completely glued.

When the whole design had been glued onto the inside of the jar and lid, I cleaned any excess glue from the backs of the prints and the glass with a piece of sponge that had been well wrung out in hot water.

When the jar was completely dry, I painted the

inside of the jar, using the sable brush and working in short strokes, spiraling from the bottom. I painted over the paper cutouts so that the brush only moved outward over the edges. I used the paint sparingly so that there was no risk of it dribbling down the sides.

I then left the first coat to dry for twenty-four hours. It looked rather rough, but the second coat smoothed everything out beautifully.

Frieze

If you fancy lifting one of your rooms out of its rut and making it uniquely yours, treat it to a custom-made and highly personalized frieze. The frolicking cherubs on my dining-room frieze are very "me" and came from a tiny black-and-white illustration in a book, which I had enlarged and printed on a photocopier.

Preparing the walls
You will need:
- Yardstick
- Chalk
- Paint for base coat
- House-painting brush
- White glue

Making the frieze
You will need:
- Black-and-white drawing, illustration or print
- Sheet of lightweight paper
- Temporary adhesive
- Sheet of heavyweight white paper or thin cardboard
- White glue
- Latex paint
- Designer's colors
- Artist's sable brushes

The original design needed a bit of cutting and re-arranging onto strips of heavyweight paper or thin cardboard and then the whole thing was painted with latex and designer's colors so that it blended in with the base coat on the walls. The painted strips were then photocopied in color several times, so that there were enough to make a continuous frieze around the room. From my point of view, the end result was very special and highly satisfactory.

The upper part of my dining room walls are painted with flat latex and the dado has an oil-based, rag-rolled finish, but any surface, including paper, is suitable for a frieze, provided it is clean and reasonably smooth.

Before I painted my walls, I had to measure exactly where the division between the plain wall and the decorated dado would occur, since I wanted to ensure that this juncture would be well covered by

1 In spite of the supposed difficulty of photo-copying pastels, I finally got mine printed and trimmed off the white edges before gluing the design in place.

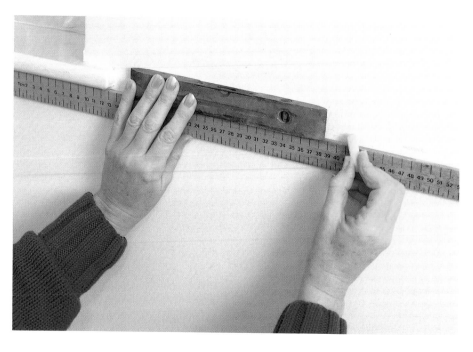

2 Luckily, my window problem was easy to solve, and using a measuring stick and a piece of chalk, I measured and marked the height of the dado all around the room.

my frieze. An added complication was that I have two windows at slightly different heights in my dining room, and I had to make sure that the frieze would not end up at an inappropriate place when it reached them.

It is almost inevitable that any room you tackle will present an architectural obstacle of some kind, but although most problems can be solved with a little ingenuity, the real trick is to recognize them before you are up to your eyeballs in them!

Luckily, my window problem was easy to solve, and using a measuring stick and a piece of chalk, I measured and marked the height of the dado all around the room. I proceeded to paint the walls, allowed them to dry thoroughly, then measured and marked lines to represent both the top and the bottom of the frieze so that I ended up with the

exact band of wall that the frieze was going to occupy.

Because part of this band was painted with latex paint, which is very porous, I sealed the whole frieze area by painting it with a mixture of one part white glue to one part water, and allowed it to dry.

You will have to do the same if your wall is covered with latex paint or if it has been wall-papered. It will not be necessary if your walls have an oil-based paint on them, however.

Color photocopying can be expensive, especially when you are making a frieze for a fairly large room. For this reason, it is a good idea if you can design your frieze so that more than one strip can be printed on the same page.

Keep in mind that photocopying machines often leave a small unprinted margin all around the page, so you shouldn't let your design completely fill the page.

When I had worked out the dimensions of my design, I drew the strips exactly to size on both the heavyweight and the lightweight paper. Then, since it was obvious that my original black-and-white illustration was going to be too small for my frieze, I had it enlarged on the photocopier to a more appropriate size.

After that, I began cutting out and arranging the design on the cartridge paper strips, moving the pieces around until I had them to my liking and holding them temporarily in place with temporary adhesive.

I also checked that the design would run smoothly from the end of one strip onto the beginning of the next with no obvious change in the sequence. When I was sure that I had the design flowing smoothly, I transferred the cutouts onto the heavyweight paper and glued them into place using a mixture of one part white glue to one part water.

As I pasted each piece on, I also gave it a coating of glue on the right side, both to seal it and to

encourage it to dry flat. When the design was completely glued on, I allowed the whole thing to dry thoroughly.

To paint the design, I first gave everything a coat of slightly diluted latex paint, which was the same color as the upper part of my wall. The paint was just thin enough to enable me to see the black-and-white design through it.

I mixed a little of the designer color into the latex so that I had a darker color with which to paint the shadowy areas of the design. I then mixed a little white into the original latex color and painted the lighter areas. I finished off by painting the extreme highlights in pure white. The result was a monochrome design that looked almost as though it was in relief.

My design was in pastel shades and, as one photocopying machine operator said to me with great feeling, "These machines hate pastels." It is true that photocopiers are far more successful with brighter colors, but I have found that it is only bad operators who really "hate pastels," and that it is worth hunting around if yours is a delicately colored design. There *are* some good printers who can do the job—if you search hard enough!

Anyway, when I finally got mine printed, I trimmed off the white edges and glued the design in place on the wall using slightly diluted white glue and the same technique of gluing the back and the front of the design as I had used when gluing it to the heavyweight paper.

The glue that I pasted onto the front of the frieze should both seal and protect the design, and there is usually no need to do anything further—except, of course, stand back and admire.

3 I mixed a little of the designer color into the latex so that I had a darker color with which to paint the shadowy areas of the design. I then mixed a little white into the original latex color and painted the lighter areas. I finished off by painting the extreme highlights in pure white. The result was a monochrome design that looked almost as though it was in relief.

Index

The United States

Aiko's Art Materials Import, Inc.
3347 North Clark Street
Chicago, IL 60657
(312) 404-5600

Basic Crafts Co.
1201 Broadway
New York, NY 10001
(212) 670-3516

Daniel Smith Inc.
4130 First Avenue South
Seattle, WA 98134
(800) 426-6740

The Paper Tree
1743 Buchanan Mall
San Francisco, CA 94115
(415) 921-7100

Pearl Paint
308 Canal Street
New York, NY 10013
(212) 431-7932

Rugg Road Paper and Prints
1 Fitchburg Street B154
Somerville, MA 02143
(617) 666-0007

Canada

Curry's Art Store Ltd.
756 Yonge Street
Toronto, Ontario M4Y 2B9
(416) 967-6666

La Papeterie St.-Armand
950 Rue Ottawa
Montreal, Quebec H3C 1S4
(514) 874-4089